The Samoan Story of Creation

By

Dr. John Fraser

First published in 1891

Published by Left of Brain Books

Copyright © 2023 Left of Brain Books

ISBN 978-1-396-32516-8

First Edition

All rights reserved. No part of this publication may be reproduced, distributed, or transmitted in any form or by any means, including photocopying, recording, or other electronic or mechanical methods, without the prior written permission of the publisher, except in the case of brief quotations permitted by copyright law. Left of Brain Books is a division of Left Of Brain Onboarding Pty Ltd.

PUBLISHER'S PREFACE

About the Book

"Samoa, officially the Independent State of Samoa, is a country governing the western part of the Samoan Islands archipelago in the South Pacific Ocean. Previous names were Samoa from 1900 to 1919, and Western Samoa from 1914 to 1997. It was admitted to the United Nations on 15 December 1976 as Samoa. The entire island group, inclusive of American Samoa, was known as Navigators Islands before the 20th century because of the Samoans' seafaring skills."

(Quote from wikipedia.org)

CONTENTS

PUBLISHER'S PREFACE
INTRODUCTION 1
TRANSLATION 10
    THE PRODUCTION OF THE NINE HEAVENS 13
    THE PRODUCTION OF OTHER GODS 14
ADDENDUM 20
ENDNOTES 22

INTRODUCTION

1. [1] All nations have traditions or speculations as to their own origin, and these often include a Cosmogony, by which they endeavour to account for the existence of the world, or at least of their own land, and for the creation of men to be its inhabitants. Our own Australian blacks, whom some ethnologists wrongly describe as the lowest of human beings, speak of a great Creator, known by such tribal names as Baiamai, Punjil, Nuralli, who made them and all things, and who still lives in the heavens above; in the work of creation, he carried a great knife, with which to shape the toil of his hands; in this work he is assisted by a demiourgos whom the Kamalarai tribe call Dharamulan, and certain birds and animals are also associated with him as agents; Punjil first made two men each of a lump of clay, which he gradually fashioned from the feet upwards into the human form; and, as the figures grew in symmetry and beauty, he danced round them, well satisfied with his work; then he breathed very hard on them and they lived, and began to move about as full-grown men. The one had straight hair, and the other had curly hair.

2. [2] Punjil's brother had control of all waters, great and small; and so, one day, he brought up by a hook from a muddy-pool two young women, and they became the companions of the two men. Some time after, Punjil came down and visited the camp of the blacks; and, becoming very angry, he used his great knife on the men, women, and children there, and cut them into very small pieces, which still lived and wriggled about like worms; these he carried into the sky, and then dropped them wherever he pleased; the pieces became men and women, and peopled the whole land. Baiamai gave to the blacks their sacred songs and their social institutions.

There is not much of a Cosmogony in this tale, for it tells us only how men were brought into being, and how Australia came to be occupied by straight-haired and curly-haired blacks; but I have introduced it here, because it bears some relation to the Polynesian myth which I am now to make known to you.

3. [3] The Polynesian race of the Eastern Pacific has an elaborate system of Cosmogony, which aims at explaining how the heavens were created and sustained, how gods and men came to be, how their own islands arose; but the details thereof vary much as given by the wise men in the various groups. Of the varying forms of the great Myth of Creation, the one I have here from Sāmoa seems to me to be the purest and the noblest, and to be the original from which the others have come. Any one who knows Polynesia would reasonably expect this to be so, for, in many respects, the Sāmoans are a nobler people than most of the other islanders; they have a strong claim to be considered the parents of the race; and their highest chiefs and priests were the depositories of the old traditions and beliefs. The present myth was communicated by one of these old chiefs, Taua-nuʻu of Manuʻa, and as Mr. Powell who got it had his full confidence, I have no doubt that this is a genuine and uncorrupted record. In estimating value, we must always bear in mind that natives consider their traditional records as property which ought not to be shared with stangers; if circumstances compel them to open their stores against their will to foreigners, they so abridge or mutilate the narrative that it is then of little value, and, only when there is mutual confidence and trust as between friends, will they consent to tell the tale in its fulness and purity. Now, it is evident that this condition of friendship existed between Taua-nuʻu and Mr. Powell. Hence my belief in the genuineness of this record.

4. [4] There is much simple dignity in the opening sentence of the myth—"The god Tangaloa dwelt in the Expanse" as the sole intelligence there. He was soon to be the creator of all things, but as yet there was no sky, no sea, no land. He moved to and fro in the Expanse.

It is noticeable that this opening sentence of the myth assumes the prior existence of three things before the work of creation began—(1) an Expanse or Firmament, (2) an intelligent and self-existing creative principle, 'le atua Tagaloa,' the god Tangaloa, and (3) the material wherewith to form the earth. There is here no notion that the earth was formed out of nothing. There is, however, an implied belief in the eternity of matter,—the matter, at least, which became the primitive papa, 'rock.' And also there was an Expanse, a sort of illimitable space—and that is a necessary belief in every creation-myth, but there was no sky, that is, no cloud-land or rain-land such as is now over the earth, and there was Tangaloa, moving to and fro at will in the Expanse. I therefore take Tangaloa to be the Aether of other cosmogonies,—the bright and pure principle of light and heat which existed before the sun, and which spread everywhere in that earliest state of things which we call Chaos. And, as this myth goes on, we shall find that, according to Polynesian belief, after the heavens and the earth had been made, this same Tangaloa places himself in the highest heavens, the Ninth, the clearest empyrean—where no cloud ever comes,—and there he dwells, calm and undisturbed, in his faleʻula, his 'palace of brightness.' So I see nothing sordid in these three Polynesian ideas; the whole presents itself to me as a very chaste opening to a Creation-myth.

In this same sense, Charles Kingsley eloquently says:—"Those simple-hearted forefathers of ours said within themselves

'Where is the All-father'? Then they lifted up their eyes to the clear, blue sky, the boundless firmament of heaven. That never changed; that was always the same. The clouds and storms rolled far below it, and all the bustle of this noisy world; but there the sky was still, as bright and calm as ever. The All-Father must be there, unchangeable in the unchanging heaven; bright, and pure, and boundless, like the heaven; and like the heavens too, silent and far off. So they named him after the heaven, Tuisco—the God who lives in the clear heaven, the heavenly father. He was the Father of Gods and men; and man was the son of Tuisco and Hertha—heaven and earth."

Now as to the meaning and derivation of the name Tangaloa, I may call to your remembrance the fact that the Anglo-Saxon god-name, Tuisco, is of the same origin as the Eng. word day and Lat. dies; the old Aryan root is dyu or div, 'to shine,' which gives other god-names, the Sans. Dyaus and deva, the Gr. Zeus and Zēn, and the Lat. Jupiter, Jovis, as well as the common noun divus. The idea common to them all is that of 'bright, lustrous, beaming,' and this fits in with the fact that Tangaloa dwells in the empyrean above. But, in seeking for a derivation of the name Tangaloa, I call to mind the Polynesian tradition that originally the sky lay flat on the lower world, lalo-langi, as they call it, the 'under-the-sky,' and that the nine heavens, being now propped up, surround the earth and envelope it on all sides. Therefore I divide the name Tangaloa into two parts tanga and loa; in Samoan the verb ta'ai, that is, takai (= tangai) means, to 'wind round' like an ulcer encircling a limb, and ta'aiga is a 'roll,' of mats or tobacco or the like. In the Maori dialect, tangai is the 'bark' or 'rind,' that which 'envelopes,' and takai is a 'wrapper'; in Samoan tanga is a 'bag,' that which 'envelopes' or 'encloses.' I would therefore say that the name was at first Tanga-la, then lengthened into Tanga-loa,—'the god that encompasses all things,' 'the encircling Aether'; but, as -la is not a common formative in Polynesian dialects, at least so far as I know, it is quite possible that -loa is a separate word, and may be the Samoan loa, 'long,' 'far off.'

5. [5] The myth next goes on to say that, in his wandering to and fro in the Expanse, Tangaloa one day stood still, and then there grew up păpă, 'a rock,' for him to rest on. In another Samoan myth, 'le Solo o le Va,' Tangaloa is, at another time, weary of flying over the waste of waters, and no sooner does he express a wish for a resting place, than an island rises up from the deep for him. In both cases, there is no laborious work of creation ascribed to him, but his wish or his need at once produces the result desired. There is certainly some dignity in this.

The word păpă, in Samoan, means 'rock,' but in other dialects it also means 'foundation,' 'anything level or flat,' and pala, means 'mud.' Now I take the myth here to indicate that, by the exercise of his will alone, Tangaloa caused to spring up, out of chaos, first the solid foundation-material out of which the Earth, the Sea, the Sky, were afterwards evolved by separate fiats or acts of creation; for the myth then declares that he spake to the Rock, saying, 'Be thou split open,' and there came forth, as if by successive efforts of parturition, various kinds of foundation-stuff, then the Earth, then the Sea, and Fresh-water, and the Sky, and 'Prince-Prop-up-sky,' and Immensity, and Space, and Height, and, last of all, Man, as a physical being, but not yet endowed with intelligence. Unlike the original papa, all of these come into existence, not at his will, but by the power of a separate command of evolution for each.

I am not much concerned to explain how, on natural principles, the Sea, and the Sky, and Man himself, can have been produced by this papa, but the succession of ideas in this Samoan myth is consistent; for first comes the Rock or Foundation—the physical origin of all things—then the varieties of rock, which are soon united to form the Earth; then the Sea, 'le tai,' is made to surround the Earth and lave its shores; then its counterpart, 'le vai,' Fresh-water, appears on the Earth; hitherto Earth and Sky had been as one, but now the Sky is lifted up above the earth and secured in its place by props; then the dimensions Length, Breadth, and Height appeared; and then, all things being ready for him, Man came upon the scene.

6. [6] But Man was yet a dull, inert mass of matter; so Tangaloa created Spirit, and Heart, and Will, and Thought, and put them within him, and thus Man became a living soul. Here the myth duly recognises the composite nature of man, and that too with a precision scarcely to be expected from Polynesians.

7. [7] The Kosmos had been, to some extent, arranged already as Land, Sea, and Sky, but now that Man is to dwell on earth, Tangaloa proceeds to make him comfortable; and so he sends Immensity and Space, as a wedded pair, to dwell in the sky above; he bids another pair, 'Two-clouds' and 'Two-fresh-water-bottles,' attend to the supply of water from the clouds, and another pair to people the Sea. Meanwhile the man and his wife are to people the earth on its southern side. But now a catastrophe seems to have happened, for Tui-te'e-langi, the Polynesian Atlas, found himself unable any longer to support the weight of the sky, and so it fell down on the earth once more. Then Tui bethought him of two native plants that grow, spread out a-top like an umbrella; with these he propped up the sky, and it has never fallen since! In this connection, it is curious to note that our Australian Aborigines believe similarly that the sky is held up by props, and they have a tradition that the props once broke, and then the wizards had great work to do in getting the sky propped up again.

8. [8] The wedded pair, Immensity and Space, that had a little before been removed from the earth to the sky, now brought forth children—Night and Day, and these two, by their united action, produced the Sun and the Stas; these two dwell in the First Heavens, the region of alternate darkness and brightness. Immensity and Space next gave birth to Le-Langi, 'the clear, blue sky'; that is the Second Heavens. Langi then produces all the other heavens up to the Ninth, and each of these is peopled by Immensity and Space. All this means that, above the cloud land of the First Heaven, everything is serene, calm, and clear, and everywhere there is illimitable extension of space. So it must have appeared, at all events, to the earliest of myth-makers, when they turned their thoughts from earth to heaven.

9. [9] Our myth now turns to the creation of the other gods; every one of these, however, is a Tangaloa, and is therefore not a seperate and independant being, but only a phase, as it were, of the supreme Tangaloa—a distinct manifestation of himself in some one or other of his functions. These he created, but the word used here fa'a-tupu, only implies that he 'caused them to grow up' or to be. Of all these facets of himself, he makes Tangaloa-le-fuli, 'the immoveable,' to be the chief, for up there, in his domain, the Ninth Heavens, the clouds 'never roll along' (le fuli), the storms below never come nigh, and all is tranquility and peace.

10. The myth next shows the Sāmoan pride of race, for it makes Sāmoa and Manu'a to be brothers to the Sun and the Moon. And yet we cannot believe that the Polynesians are akin to the rulers of the Celestial Empire. After these, the other islands of the Pacific, as known to Sāmoans,—Tonga and Fiji and the Eastern groups—are made to spring up at the will of 'Tangaloa-the-creator-of-lands.' This is a much more dignified account of things than that which is given in some other Polynesian legends, which say that, while one of the gods was engaged in fishing in the sea, he pulled up with his line an island here and

there; and that had not the line at last broken with the pull, some of these islands might have been continents.

11. [10] But the newly-created islands are, as yet, rough and rugged and unfit for the occupation of man; and so 'Tangaloa-the-creator' comes down and treads upon them, and prepares them for people to dwell in. And he looked on all his work, and said, 'It is good.' To people these lands, he causes Tangaloa-sāváli to take a native climbing-plant, a Fue, and lay it outside in the sun. Under the Sun's heat, its juice brought forth a great multitude of worms; these Tangaloa fashioned into men and women, and gave them intelligence, and thus he peopled the lands. This Fue must represent some echo of the original creation of mankind by God, for our myth says, at its close, that Fue was the son of Tangaloa, and there is still in Sāmoa a variety of this vine, which is called Fue-sā, the 'sacred vine.' And, to Sāmoans, such origination of life is intelligible; for they have experience of animal life as a product of the sun's heat, to procure oil, they slice their cocoa-nuts into lumps, and leaving a heap of this 'copra' exposed in a canoe, they find that it soon produces oil and worms.

12. [11] As a parallel to this account of the origin of man, I now refer to the Australian tradition with which I began this introduction. There the creation-god is Baiamai, that is, Bai-bai, an intensive and therefore honorific name, formed from the Australian root-word ba, 'to cause to be,' 'to make'; similarly, the verb punjilko, that is, punjil with the infinitive suffix -ko added, means 'to cut out,' 'to shape,' 'to make'; hence Baimai and Punjil simply mean 'the creator.' In his creative work, Punjil uses a knife wherewith to shape all things; similarly Tangaloa cuts and shapes the vine-worms 'into member'd forms.' Punjil too, when he wishes the land to be occupied, cuts the people into small worm-like pieces and scatters them about. Tangaloa declares himself well pleased with his handiwork; Punjil, in delight, dances around the clay image of the man which he was making. Tangaloa gives spirit and heart to animate man; Punjil breathes hard on his image and the man lives, Tangaloa, in one of his aspects, is the lord of the sea; Punjil's brother is the lord of all waters. Baiamai gave to the Australians all their socal regulations; so also, among the Polynesians, all authority comes from Tangaloa; he gave them kingly rule, and the right of holding councils, and enjoined them to live in peace.

And thus, in folk-lore and in tradition myths, parallel stories may be found in the most unlikely quarters, all the world over and these parallels can scarcely have proceeded from merely a similar power of invention in so many diverse nations; they seem to indicate a common origin.

TRANSLATION

13. [12] The god Tangaloa dwelt in the Expanse; he made all things; he alone was [there]; not any sky, not any country; he only went to and fro in the Expanse; there was also no sea, and no earth; but, at the place where he stood there grew up a rock. Tangaloa-fa'a-tutupu-nu'u was his name; all things were about to be made, by him, for all things were not yet made; the sky was not made nor any thing else; but there grew up a Rock on which he stood.

14. [13] Then Tangaloa said to the Rock, 'Be thou split up.' Then was brought forth Papa-taoto; after that, Papa-sosolo; then Papa-lau-a'au; then Papa-'ano-'ano; then Papa-'ele; then Papa-tu; then Papa-'amu-'amu and his children.

15. [14] But Tangaloa stood facing the west, and spoke to the Rock. Then Tangaloa struck the Rock with his right hand, and it split open towards the right side. Then the Earth was brought forth (that is the parent of all the people in the world), and the Sea was brought forth. Then the Sea covered the Papa-sosolo; and Papa-nofo [that is, Papa-taoto] said to Papa-sosolo, 'Blessed are you in [the possession of] your sea.' Then said Papa-sosolo 'Don't bless me; the sea will soon reach you too.' All the rocks in like manner called him blessed.

16. [15] Then Tangaloa turned to the right side, and the Freshwater sprang up. Then Tangaloa spake again to the Rock, and the Sky was produced. He spake again to the Rock and Tui-te'e-langi was brought forth; then came forth Ilu, 'Immensity,' and Mamao, 'Space,' came (that was a woman); then came Niuao.

17. [16] Tangaloa spake again to the Rock; then Lua'o, a boy, came forth. Tangaloa spake again to the Rock, and Lua-vai, a girl, came forth. Tangaloa appointed these two to the Sā-tua-langi.

18. [17] Then Tangaloa spoke again, and Aoa-lālā, a boy was born, and [next] Ngao-ngao-le-tai, a girl; then came Man; then came the Spirit; then the Heart; then the Will; then Thought.

19. [18] That is the end of Tangaloa's creations which were produced from the Rock; they were only floating about on the sea[19]; there was was no fixedness there.

20. [20] Then Tangaloa made an ordinance to the rock and said:—

(1) Let the Spirit and the Heart and Will and Thought go on and join together inside the Man; and they joined together there and man became intelligent. And this was joined to the earth ('ele-ele'), and it was called Fatu-ma-le-'Ele-'ele, as a couple,[21] Fatu the man, and 'Ele-'ele, the woman.

(2) Then he said to Immensity and Space, 'Come now; you two be united up above in the sky with your boy Niuao, then they went up; there was only a void, nothing for the sight to rest upon.

(3) Then he said to Lua-'o and Lua-vai, 'Come now, you two, that the region of fresh-water may be peopled.'

(4) But he ordains Aoa-lālā and Ngao-ngao-le-tai to the sea, that they two may people the sea.

(5) And he ordains Le-Fatu and Le-'Ele-'ele, that they people this side; he points them to the left-hand side, opposite to Tua-langi.

(6) Then Tangaloa said to Tui-te'e-langi, 'Come here now; that you may prop up the sky.' Then it was propped up; it reached up on high. But it fell down because he was not able for it. Then Tui-te'e-langi went to Masoa and Teve; he brought them and used them as props; then he was able. (The masoa and the teve were the first plants that grew, and other plants came afterwards). Then the sky remained up above, but there was nothing for the sight to rest upon. There was only the far-receding sky, reaching to Immensity and Space.

THE PRODUCTION OF THE NINE HEAVENS

21. [22] Then Immensity and Space brought forth offspring; they brought forth Po and Ao, 'Night and Day,' and this couple was ordained by Tangaloa to produce the 'Eye of Sky,' [the Sun]. Again Immensity and Space brought forth Le-Langi; that is the Second Heavens; for Tui-te'e-langi went forth to prop it up and the sky became double; and Immensity and Space remained there, and they peopled the sky. Then again Langi brought forth, and Tui-te'e-langi went forth and propped it up; that was the Third Heavens; that was peopled by Immensity and Space. Then Langi bore again; that was the Fourth Heavens. Tui-te'e-langi went forth to prop it up; that heaven also was peopled by Ilu and Mamao. Then Langi bore again; that was the Fifth Heavens. Then went forth Tui-te'e-langi to prop it up; that heaven also was peopled by Ilu and Mamao. Langi brought forth again; that was the Sixth Heavens. And Tui-te'e-langi went and propped it up; that heaven was peopled by Ilu and Mamao. Then Langi bore again; that was the Seventh Heavens. And Tui-te'e-langi went forth and propped it up; that heaven was peopled by Ilu and Mamao. Then Langi again brought forth; that was called the Eighth Heavens. Tui-te'e-langi went to prop up that heaven; and that heaven was peopled by Ilu and Mamao. Then again Langi brought forth; that was the Ninth Heavens; and it was propped up by Tui-te'e-langi; and that heaven was peopled by Ilu and Mamao. Then ended the productiveness of Ilu and Mamao; it reached to the Ninth Heavens.

THE PRODUCTION OF OTHER GODS

22. [23] Then Tangaloa sat [still]; he is well known as Tangaloa-faʻa-tutupu-nuʻu; then he created Tangaloa-lē-fuli, and Tangaloa-asiasi-nuʻu, and Tangaloa-tolo-nuʻu, and Tangaloa-sāváli, and Tuli also, and Longonoa.

23. Then said Tangaloa, the creator, to Tangaloa-lē-fuli, 'Come here; be thou chief in the heavens.' Then Tangaloa, 'the immoveable,' was chief in the heavens.

24. [24] Then Tangaloa, the creator, said to Tangaloa-sāváli, 'the messenger,' 'Come here; be thou ambassador in all the heavens, beginning from the Eighth Heavens down to the First Heavens, to tell them all to gather together in the Ninth Heavens, where Tangaloa, the immoveable, is chief. Then proclamation was made that they should go up to the Ninth Heavens, and then visit below the children of Night and Day in the First Heavens.

25. [25] Then Tangaloa, the messenger, went down to Night and Day in the First Heavens, and asked them thus:—'Have you two any children appointed to you? And they answered, 'Come here; these two are our children, appointed to us, Langi-ʻuli and Langi-mā.'

26. [26] All the stars also were their offspring, but we do not have the names of all the stars (the stars had each it own name), for they are forgotten now, because they dropped out of use. And surely the last injunction of Tangaloa, the creator, to Night and Day was that they should produce the Eye-of-the-Sky. That was the reason Tangaloa, the messenger, went down to ask Night and Day in the First Heavens [if they had any children].

27. [27] Then answered Night and Day, 'Come now; there remain four boys that are not yet appointed,—Manu'a, Sāmoa, the Sun, and the Moon.'

28. [28] These are the boys that originated the names of Sāmoa and Manu'a; these two were the children of Night and Day. The name of the one is Sā-tia-i-le-moa, 'obstructed by the chest'; the meaning of which is this:—the boy seemed as if he would not be born, because he was caught by the chest; therefore it was he was called Sā-tia-i-le-moa, that is, Sāmoa; the other was born with one side abraded ('manu'a'); then said Day to Night 'Why is this child so greatly wounded?' therefore the child was called 'Manu'a-tele.'

29. Then said Tangaloa, the messenger, 'It is good; come now; go up into the Ninth Heavens, you four; all are about to gather together there to form a Council; go up you two also.' Then they all gathered together in the Ninth Heavens,—the place where dwelt Tangaloa, the creator, and Tangaloa, the immoveable; the Council was held in the Ninth Heavens; the ground where they held the Council was Malaē-a-Toto'a, 'the council ground of Tranquillity.'

30. [29] Then various decrees were made in the Ninth Heavens; the children of Ilu and Mamoa were appointed all of them to be builders, and to come down from the Eighth Heavens to this [earth] below; perhaps they were ten thousand in all that were appointed to be builders; they had one name all were [called] Tangaloa. Then they built houses for the Tangaloa; but the builders did not reach to the Ninth Heavens—the home of Tangaloa-lē-fuli—which was called the 'Bright House' [fale-'ula].

31. Then said Tangaloa, the creator, to Night and Day:—'Let those two boys go down below to be chiefs over the offsprings of Fatu and 'Ele-'ele.' But to the end of the names of the two boys was attached the name of Tangaloa-lē-fuli who is king ('tupu') of the Ninth Heavens; hence the [Samoan] kings ('tupu') were named 'Tui o Manu'a-tele ma Samoa atoa.'

32. [30] Then Tangaloa, the creator, said to Night and Day:—'Let those two boys, the Sun and the Moon, go and follow you two; when day comes, let the Sun follow; also when Night comes, the Moon too comes on.' These two are the shades of Tangaloa; they are well-known in all the world; the Moon is the shade of Tangaloa; but thus runs the decree of Tangaloa, the creator,— Let there be one portion of the heavens, in which they pass along; in like manner also shall the Stars pass along.'

33. [31] Then Tangaloa, the messenger, went to and fro to visit the land; his visit began in the place where are (now) the Eastern groups; these groups were made to spring up; then he went off to cause the group of Fiji to grow up; but the space between seemed so far off that he could not walk it; then he stood there and turned his face to the Sky, [praying] to Tangaloa, the creator, and Tangaloa, the immoveable; Tangaloa looked down to Tangaloa, the messenger; and he made the Tongan group spring up; then that land sprang up.

34. [32] Then he turns his face to this Manu'a; and looks up to the heavens, for he is unable to move about; then Tangaloa, the creator and Tangaloa, the immovable, looked down, and caused Savai'i to spring up; then that land grew up.

35. [33] Then Tangaloa, the messenger, went back to the heavens, and said—'We have (now) got countries, the Eastern group and the Fiji group, and the Tongan group, and Savai'i.' Then, as all these lands were grown up, Tangaloa, the creator, went down in a black cloud to look at the countries, and he delighted in them; and he said, 'It is good;' then he stood on the top of the mountains to tread them down, that the land might be prepared for people to dwell in. Then he returned [on high]. And Tangaloa, the creator, said [to Tangaloa, the messenger],— 'Come now; go back by the road you came; take people to possess the Eastern groups; take Atu and Sasaʻe; that is a pair; they were called conjointly Atu-Sasae; these two people came from the heavens from among the children of Tangaloa.

36. Then Tangaloa, the messenger, went again to the Fiji group; he also again took two persons, a pair—their names were Atu and Fiji—from among all the children of Tangaloa; so that group of islands was called Atu-Fiji.

37. Then he turned his face towards Tonga; he took [with him] a couple; their names were Atu and Tonga; these two peopled that group of islands; their names were the Atu-Tonga; these two were the people of Tangaloa.

38. [34] Then Tangaloa, the messenger, came back to this Manuʻa, to Le-Fatu and Le-ʻEle-ʻele and their children; because the command of Tangaloa, the creator, [had gone forth] from the heavens, that Le-Fatu and Le-ʻEle-ʻele should go there to people this side of the world. Then went out Valuʻa and Tiʻăpă to people Savaiʻi; these two are the children of Le-Fatu and Le-ʻEle-ʻele; these two people are from this Manuʻa; Savaiʻi and this Manuʻa are one; these two were the parents of Iʻi and Sava; Iʻi was the girl, and Sava was the boy; that island was peopled by them, and was named Savaiʻi.

39. [35] And Tangaloa, the messenger, went again to this Manuʻa; then he stood and faced the sky, as if he were making a prayer;

then Tangaloa, the creator looked down, and the land of Upólu sprang up. Then Tangaloa, the messenger, stood and again faced the heavens towards Tangaloa, the creator; and Tangaloa, the creator, looked down from the heavens, and the land of Tutuila sprang up.

40. [36] Then Tangaloa, the messenger, turned to the heavens, and said, 'Two lands are now gotten for me to rest in. And Tangaloa, the creator, said, 'Come now, go you with the Peopling-vine; take it and place it outside in the sun; leave it there to bring forth; when you see it has brought forth, tell me.' Then he took it and placed it in Salēa-au-mua, a council-ground, which is now called the Malae-of-the-sun. Then Tangaloa, the messenger, was walking to and fro; and he visited the place where the Fue was; he went there and it had brought forth. Then he went back again to tell Tangaloa, the creator, that the Fue had brought forth. Then Tangaloa, the creator, first went down; he went to it; he looked, and it had brought forth something like worms; wonderful was the multitude of worms; then Tangaloa, the creator, shred them into stripes, and fashioned them into members, so that the head, and the face, and the hands, and the legs were distinguishable; the body was now complete, like a man's body; he gave them heart and spirit; four persons grew up; so this land was peopled; there grew up Tele and Upólu, which are the children of the Fue; Tutu and Ila, that is a pair; these are the children of Fue; four persons, Tele and Upólu, Tutu and Ila. Tele and Upólu were placed to people the land of Upolu-tele; but Tutu and Ila, they two were to people the land now called Tutuila.

41. Fue, the son of Tangaloa, that came down from heaven, had two names, Fue-tangata and Fue-sa; he peopled the two flat lands.

42. [37] Then Tangaloa gave his parting command thus; 'Always show respect to Manuʻa; if any one do not, he will be overtaken by calamity; but let each one do as he likes with his own lands.'

43. [38] [Here] the story of the creation of Sāmoa finishes with this parting command, which was given at Malae-lā.

ADDENDUM

THE Mexican story of Creation may be compared with the Polynesian 'tala;' I therefore quote a few points of resemblance from a French translation of the "Codex Ramirez," which was written in Spanish soon after the conquest of Mexico: "The first god and the first goddess were self-created, and dwelt in the Third Heavens; of their four sons, one was born red, another was born black.[39] Two of these sons, by appointment, proceeded to create first fire, then a half-sun, then a man and a woman, then the days, then a great fish[40] like a cayman, out of which they made the earth. As yet there was no division of time into years; so the creating gods now made a full sun to shine on the earth. Then great giants were made, who lived only on acorns, and could carry trees in their hands. Soon after it rained[41] so much that the sky fell down upon the earth. The gods then created four men to help them to raise the sky again, and two of the gods changed themselves into trees[42] for the same end. The Sun now resumed his place in the sky, and, in order that he might have hearts to feed on,[43] and blood to drink, men were compelled to engage in perpetual war. One year after this one of the four gods took a rod, and with it struck a rock, from which sprang the 'mountaineers,' who occupied the country before the Mexicans came there."

In the introduction to this 'tala,' I have offered a new derivation of the name Tangaloa. I wish now to add that that derivation has some support from what we know as the Vedic god Varuna—the same word as the Greek ouranos, 'heaven.' The name Varuna is derived from the Sanskrit verb veri, 'to cover,' 'to surround;' and, in its compounds, 'to enclose,' 'to overspread;' a participial noun from it means 'a wrapper,' 'a cloak;' with these compare the Polynesian words already cited. In the Veda Varuna is one of the most ancient of deities; he is sprung from 'Space,' and is the god of the heavens; in some of the later hymns he is regarded as controlling the waters, both in heaven and on earth; hence in the later mythologgy his name is synonymous with 'the waters,' 'the ocean.' For, just as the Vedic Varuna covers and encompasses the terrestrial sphere, so the Homeric mighty river Okeanos surrounds the whole of the terrestrial lands. With all this compare the functions of Tangaloa, who, in some localities in Polynesia, is also lord of the sea.

In the Greek mythology, Ouranos is the grandfather of Zeus, and Varuna is thus more venerable and ancient than Dyaus, the lower sky.

ENDNOTES

[1] Punjil; for an account of Punjil and his works, see R. Brough Smyth's "Aborigines of Victoria," Vol. I., and for Baiamai, see Ridley's "Kamilaroi."

Baiamai; in the text I have given this form of the name, for it is the common one; but I think that it ought to be written Ba-ye-mai; for ba is the root 'to make,' ba-yé means 'one who makes,' and mai is a formative termination.

Kamalarai; this name for a native language and tribe in New South Wales has always been written Kamilaroi; but the composition of the word requires the spelling Kámălarai, for it is made up of ka (dialect kya) 'not,' -mal and -araiʻ which are common formative suffixes.

Dhara-mulan; a demiurge figures in many of the ancient cosmogonies. The Egyptian demiurge Thoth created light for the world, while as yet there was no sun, and in the Orphic hymns, light exists before the sun; cf. note 4 s. v. Aether. In the Kamalarai legends, Dhara-mulan seems to have a two-fold aspect, and hence the -mulan in his name may be the word bula, 'two.'

Breathed very hard; cf. "He breathed into his nostrils the breath of life." The Polynesian here and in other respects agrees with the Egyptian and the Hebrew Cosmogonies, which commence with chaos, regard light as anterior to the sun, postulate the moulding hand of a deity in creation and a divine breath as the source of life. The Polynesian cosmogony has also, the idea of the unity of God; for the gods are all Tangaloa. It agrees with the Avesta in tracing creation to the will of a deity and in ascribing perfection—"it is good"—to the thing created; Ahuramazda is the sole creator who made heaven and earth and men. In India also, the Self-existing One by a thought made the waters. The Babylonian Cosmogony considers water as the primal element from which life came; the Polynesian does not. (p. 1)

[2]. Punjil's brother; cf. the relation of Zeus to Poseidon.

Cut into pieces; cf. the Hebrew verb bârâ, 'to create,' which properly means 'to fashion,' 'to shape.'

Worms; cf. a subsequent note on Fue-tagata. (p. 1)

[3] The details thereof; for these, see Rev. Dr. Gill's "Myths and Songs" and Sir George Grey's "Polynesian Mythology." (p. 2)

[4]Le atua Tagaloa; this expression shows that this myth is not modern; for the word atua, 'god,' was almost obsolete when the first missionaries went to Samoa.

Aether; some commentators on Gen., I., 1-2 assert that the Ancient Jews believed the sky to be a solid vault, but that in its original state (verse 1) it was a liquid expanse; the 'separation' of the material of heaven and earth took place on the second day of creation (verses 6-8).

Envelopes; the Polynesian conception of the Heavens does not seem to include a belief that they encompass the world all round like a circle—not spheres, but crescent-shaped vaults. This also is the Hebrew notion; cf. "He that sitteth upon the circle of the earth; that stretcheth out the heavens as a curtain, and spreadeth them out as a tent to dwell in" (Is. xl., 22). "He walketh in the circuit of heaven" (Job. xxii., 14).

Fale-ula; cf. the 'Solo o le Va.' (p. 3)

[5]Papa; not a 'rock' in our sense of the word, but merely 'something flat and solid'; cf. Gen. I., 6-8. In the sense of 'foundation,' papa has numerous correspondences in the Hebrew Scriptures; cf. Isaiah xxxi.,

17, "the earth's foundation quake"—the foundations which support the visible frame of the earth.

Separate fiats; this cosmogony is thus theistical, not pantheistical.

Prince Prop-up-sky; Tui-te'e-langi; his place here, among the physioal creations of Tangaloa, shows that he is not a god—not a Tangaloa,—but a sort of physical Atlas.

The sky is lifted up; cf. the English word 'heaven' and the Scotch, 'lift.' (p. 5)

[6] Dull, inert mass; it had the worm-life from the Fue-sā, but that was all. (p. 6)

[7] Southern side; the limited knowledge which the ancients had of geography led them to regard the north as hyperborean; and thus the south was to them the habitable part of the globe. (p. 6)

[8] Sun and stars; so also in Genesis I., the sun does not appear till the fourth day. In our myth, there is no mention of the moon till further on. (p. 6)

[9] Ninth Heavens; 'three times three'; cf. the notes on this point in the 'Solo o le Va.' In the "Records of the past," we read of the 'nine gods, the masters of things,' and of a 'holy nine.' As the basis of their numeration, the Polynesians have—one, two, three; they have no knowledge of seven as a perfect number.

Tranquillity and peace; cf. the notes on this point in the 'Solo o le Va.' (p. 7)

[10] Outside in the sun; cf. the reverence given to the scarabæus, as a product of the Nile mud under the heat of the sun.

Fashioned into men; cf. Heb. bârâ, as above. (p. 8)

[11] Into member'd forms; see the 'Solo o le Va.' (p. 8)

[12] The god Tangaloa. He is the great god of the Polynesians; cf. the notes on 'Solo o le Va.' (p. 10)

[13] Be thou split open; 'māvae ia,' said of parturition; māvae, 'to open as a crack;' hence māvava, 'to yawn.'

Brought forth; the word is fanau, which is also applied to the extrusion of gum from trees. The next acts of creation are in the text expressed in each case, by toe fanau, 'again it brought forth,' but, for brevity, our translation says only 'after that;' 'then.' With fanau compare: "Before the mountains were brought forth." (Heb. yullād)—Psalm xc., 2.

Papa, 'rock;' it also means 'plain, level, flat,' and that meaning is in harmony with the 'spread out' of the note above. To the Polynesian myth-makers, their mountains, being mostly volcanic, do not belong the earliest stages of creation. The various kinds of 'papa' are indicated by the epithets attached—viz., ta'oto, 'to lie down;' sosolo, 'to run,' 'to spread like creeping-plants;' lau-a'au, 'resembling a flat reef' (a'au is a 'reef,' and to 'swim:' lau denotes uniformity); 'ano-'ano is 'honey-comb;' 'ele is a sort of volcanic mud or shale, so soft that it can be cut with an axe; tu means 'to stand' (its derivative, tugā, means 'standing in the way,' as a rock in the middle of the road); 'amu-'amu is a kind of 'branching coral,' branching like fingers.

Children; the word here is pau, not fanau, 'offspring.' (p. 10)

[14] Facing the west; in the ancient auguries and other ceremonials, the position of the celebrant was important.

Towards the right. Mr. Powell says here—"In the direction of tualagi, 'the back of the sky' the north," cf. Ovid Meta I. 2, 45. 'Right' and 'left' are equivalent to 'north' and 'south,' cf. Ps. lxxxix., 12; Is. liv., 8. To the Kelts of Sootland and Ireland, the 'right' hand is still the 'south' hand (deas for deaks, 'right;' cf. Gr. dex-ios, Lat. dex-ter, 'right'); because when the face is turned towards the east, the south is on the right. An old custom among them—said to have come down from the Druids—is called deas-iùil, 'a turn to the right;' because, in all their solemn processions, the company, in order to secure a blessing, turns to the right, and, keeping the object on the right, marches round it 'three times' in the same direction as the daily course of the sun. The motion in a contrary way is car-tual, and is considered unlucky; in Lowland Scotch this is called a widder-sins motion.

World; lalo-lagi, 'under-the-sky.'

Earth; 'ele-'ele; this is a reduplication of 'ele, 'red-earth,' 'rust,' 'dirt,' 'blood;' see 'ele-'ele. It is interesting to remember here that the Hebrew word adâmâh (cf. Adam), 'the earth,' 'the tilled ground,' comes from a root meaning to be 'red,' and is applied also to the 'dust' which mourners use.

That is the parent, &c. With this compare, "And the Lord God formed man of the dust of the ground."

The sea; sami, 'the salt water' (Lat. sal), not tai. In Genesis i., 10, as here also, 'the seas' (Heb. yâmim) are gathered together when the dry land (Heb. yâbésh, 'anything that is dried up or becomes dry') appears. The Samoan word tai means 'the sea, the tide;' the distinction between it and sami seems to be that tai is the sea where it flows upon the land, but sami is the big salt ocean.

Papa-nofo probably is 'the rock (or rocks) that remained' uncovered. The idea of the myth-maker here seems to be that the sami at first had not depth of water enough to cover anything but the papa-sosolo; but that ere long the waters would rise and reach the other rocks also, and so make them happy (amuia, 'blessed,' used in congratulations). (p. 10)

[15]Fresh-water, 'vai;' as in the 'Solo o le Va,' so here; the vai comes immediately after the tai.

Your sea. The word here is tai; cf. the note on sami.

Brought forth; produced; come forth; in the text these are always 'fanau.'

Sky; 'lagi;' pronounced langi (i = Italian i). Everywhere, the Samoan g = ng. A cognate word is the Melanesian laga, 'clear.'

Tui-te'e-lagi; tui, 'a high chief, a prince, a king;' te'e, 'to prop up;' lagi, 'the sky.' The Australian blacks also know that the sky is propped up; once the props broke, and the wizards (koráji) had the utmost difficulty in putting things right again.

Ilu, &c.; these three, Ilu, Mamao, and Niuao do not come into existence till after the sky is propped up: hence mamao, as I think, must mean 'limited extension' or 'space' from horizon to horizon, from sunrise to sunset; niuao is formed from niu, 'a cocoa-nut tree;' the Samoans say of a very tall man that he 'a walking cocoa-nut tree;' of smoke they say fa'a-niu tu, 'it stands like a cocoa-nut tree;' and in the Samoan Bible the missionaries have applied the expression to the 'pillar of fire' in the wilderness; and so, I think, that niuao must mean 'height.' The Samoan word ilu means 'innumerable,' 100,000, or any vast number; in its place in the text it cannot well refer to the stars in the sky; we may translate it 'immensity,' and apply it to distance from north to south. Ilu, Mamao, and Niuao would thus be the three dimensions formed by the bounding sky—viz., Length, Breadth, and Height, each of them, however, limited by the sky. Cf. the note on the Expanse. (p. 10)

[16] Lua'o and Luavai; lua-vai means 'two fresh-waters;' lua'o should, I think, be luao, for luā-ao, 'two clouds.'

Sā-tua-lagi; the 'race' at the 'back' of the 'sky;' the north. (p. 11)

[17] Ngao-ngao-le-tai. 'the desolate sea.'

'Came;' 'came forth;' the text has still the same toe fanau, 'again was brought forth.'

Man; 'tangata,' the human race. Last to be created was man, and the elements which are joined together to make up his composite being. These are—anga-nga, 'the spirit,' probably from the same root as nga'e, 'to breathe hard;' hence the 'breath,' the 'spirit,' in the same sense as the Heb. ruāch, Gr. psuche, Lat. spiritus, animus, Sans. âtman; in Samoan anga-nga also means 'a disembodied spirit'—loto, the 'heart or affections,' not the physical heart—finagalo 'the will,' also the 'liver;' finagalo is a word used only to chiefs; finagaloa means, 'to be angry,' 'choleric.' The next name, masalo, properly means 'doubt,' but this appears to be a secondary meaning, for 'doubt' arises from that power which enables the mind to cast things to and fro in reflection, and hence to deliberate; masalo is therefore here taken to be 'thought,' 'the power of thought.' These four Tangaloa causes to go within man's physical frame, and combine there; and thus man becomes 'intelligent, wise,' See also Ovid, Meta i., 1.

In Is. xlii., 5—the verse already quoted—the breath and the spirit (neshâmâh and ruāch) are distinguished; the one is the animal spirit or life; the other is the spirit which gives consciousness. Similarly, the Melanesians and Polynesians believe that man has two spirits—the one may leave him for a time when he is dreaming or in a faint; the other finally leaves his body at death. (p. 11)

[18] No fixture; ua leai se mea a mau ai, 'there was no thing to be fast to;' ope-opea, 'they floated about.' Cf. "The earth was without form and void;" cf. also Ovid, Meta, i., 1. (p. 11)

[19] Compare with this the story of Kahu's discovery of the Chatham Islands: "On the arrival of the Kahu at this island (Chatham Island) he found it floating about; it was Kahu who closed (fixed) all this island, including Pitt Island." There are other Polynesian myths of the same character.—EDITORS. (p. 11)

[20] An ordinance; 'tofiga.' This word comes from the verb tofi, 'to divide an inheritance,' 'to apportion a father's property among children.' Tangaloa's tofiga is thus the exercise of his sovereign pleasure in

allotting to his children their several stations and spheres of action, as indicated in the five paragraphs which follow.

Intelligent, 'atamai.' As a verb this word means 'to understand;' as an adjective, 'clever, intelligent, sensible;' as a noun, 'the mind.' The Samoan ata denotes the incorporeal shadow or spirit, as opposed to the substance of a thing; and atamai may be a derivative from it; so also the French esprit and spirituel are related. The Sanskrit âtman also means 'the breath, the soul, the undertanding,' and its derivative âtmavant means 'sensible,' 'self-controlled;' âtman is supposed to be derived from a root ava, vâ; with which compare the Heb. hâvâ 'to breathe.'

Fatu-ma-le-‘ele‘ele; 'seed-stone and earth.' Fatu is a word which, in various forms, is found in all Malaysia, Melanesia, and Polynesia, in the sense of 'hard,' 'anything hard,' 'the hard kernel or seed-stone of fruit.' For the meaning of le-‘ele‘ele, see above; but Le-‘Ele‘ele is here regarded as a woman, who, by the ordinance (tofiga) of Tangaloa is united (fa‘a-tasi, 'joined,' lit. 'made-one') to Fatu, the completed man. Fatu is the seed-giving principle, and Le ‘Ele‘ele is the receptacle of the seed. With this compare the tales in classic authors about De-métér ('Mother-earth') and Zeus.

A void; 'va-nimo-nimo;' see note above. To rest upon; lit. 'to reach to.' All this corresponds with the Heb. 'tohu' (chaos) of creation—a waste in which nothing was defined.

Region; itu, 'a side,' 'a district;' itu i matū, 'the north;' cf. Heb. 'the sides of the north,' yârekâthaim tzâphôn (Isaiah xiv., 13) where tzâphôn is the region of 'darkness' (cf. Homer, pros zophon, Odys. ix., 25) 'the north quarter,' and yârekâthaim is a dual form to mean 'both sides,' hence 'the buttocks,' 'the back,' 'the remotest parts of a country.' This agrees with the idea conveyed by tua-lagi 'the back of the sky,' to which Lua‘o and Luavai were appointed, to be regents there. Fresh-water is 'vai.' In the 'Solo o le Va,' line 21, the creation of vai and tai is mentioned. The Polynesians believed that there were reservoirs of fresh-water up in the sky. In the Biblical account of the great Flood, it is said that 'the windows of heaven were opened.'

Le Fatu: see note above. Ordains; 'tofia;' cf. ordinance, 'tofiga.'

Points; tusi, 'to point out' with the index finger.

Masoa and Teve are both referred to in the 'Solo o le Va,' lines 73, 75. The Masoa (Tacca pinnatifida) is the arrow-root tree; growing on a succulent stem, with leaves only at the top, where they spread out like the surface of a round table. The Teve (Tacca amorphophallus) is another kind of arrow-root tree, very like the Masoa. From their shape they are well fitted for the purpose to which they are applied in these myths. See also Sir Geo. Grey's "Polynesian Mythology."

There was nothing, &c.; 'a na leai se mea e taunu'u i ai le va'ai.'

Far-receding sky; 'va-nimo-nimo.' See notes above. (p. 11)

[21] NOTE.—Mr. Powell's manuscript, under date March 21, 1871, has this note:—"To-day Taua-nu'u has explained to me the reason of his reluctance to disclose his traditions; he is afraid lest contention arise, when it is found that they place Savai'i and Upólu in a position inferior to his own islands of Manu'a. When I promised due care, he opened his treasures more fully. He states that (1) 'Ele-'ele is distinct from Fatu-ma-le-'Ele-'ele; that was the name given to the first man, who was only at first floating about on the waters with 'Ele-'ele. Fatu-ma-le-'Ele-'ele was formed by the union of Spirit, Heart, Will, and Thought, and was appointed to people the lands in conjunction with 'Ele-'ele 'Earth,' but Le-'Ele-'ele was different, and Fatu was different from 'Ele-'ele. (p. 11)

[22] They brought forth; the text has 'ua fanau Ao, toe fanau Po;' another reading is, 'ua fanau Po ma Ao, ua fa'a-tagata-ina ai le lagi,' 'they brought forth Night and Day, who caused-to-be-peopled the sky.' The order Po ma Ao, 'Night and Day,' is more consonant with the ideas of the Polynesians who counted by nights. The word fa'atagataina

consists of fa'a the causative prefix already noticed, and tagata, 'man,' 'mankind,' which in another dialect is kanaka, now commonly applied to the 'labour-men' who are brought from the islands of the South Seas to the northern parts of Australia.

The eye of the sky; 'le mata o le lagi.' The Malays call the Sun mata-ari, 'the eye of the day.' The Egyptian City, On, (Heb. 'Ir-ha-Heres, Gr. Heliopolis) 'the city of the Sun,' got its name from Ain, Oin, 'the eye'—the emblem of the Sun.

The second heavens. Here the Polynesians believe, like other nations of old, that the sky originally lay flat on the earth, and covered it; by the aid of the Masoa and the Teve, Tui-te'e-lagi props it up, and this gives room for Ilu and Mamao to work; this is the First Heavens; in it are placed the Sun, and Night, and Day. Ilu and Mamao then bear again, and the Sky ('le lagi'), according to myth, is produced; this probably means the region above the clouds, for the Polynesian myth-makers must have noticed the difference between cloud-land and higher sky; this Tui propped up, and it was the Second Heavens.

Remained there—i.e., in the Third Heavens, which they peopled. The heavens above the Third are, in the myth, produced (fanau) by Langi, the 'sky' personified, but they were all peopled by Ilu and Mamao. The notion that the stars in the heavens are gods, and men, and beasts, and trees, &c., is a very old one. (p. 13)

[23] Tangaloa sat still. In the 'Solo o le Va,' he is represented as a quiet, contemplative god, who delights in tranquillity and peace—the Polynesian Brahmā, the origin and source of all things. In his active manifestations he is fa'a-tutupu-nuu (see note on par. 13), 'the creator of lands;' but in his dealings with men he works by intermediary emanations from himself, which are all of them persons, and called Tangaloa; le fuli is the 'immoveable' (le 'not,' fuli, 'to turn over,' 'to capsize'); asi-asi-nu'u, 'the omnipresent' (asi, 'to visit;' asi-asi, a frequentative; nu'u, 'a district, a country, a people'); tolo-nu'u, 'the extender of lands, or peoples' (tolo, 'to spread out;' it applies to reefs that run out into the sea, branches that spread out from the tree, or

roots running along on the surface of the ground); sāváli, 'the ambassador or messenger' (sāváli means 'to walk').

Tuli and Longonoa both mean 'deaf' or 'deafness,' but that meaning cannot apply to these workers of Tangaloa. In the 'Solo o le Va,' Tuli is the bird 'ata' or emblem of Tangaloa; so also here, I believe. As to Longonoa, the simple verb logo, means 'to report;' hence I take Longonoa to be 'the reporter,' the one who carries tidings up to Tangaloa; logonoa means 'to hear,' and logo-logoā is 'famous, renowned.' Logonoa would thus be used as a verbal adjective; and in form it corresponds with such verbs as tala-noa from tala. The Longo-noa here may be the same as the Rongo of other islands. (p. 14)

[24] They should go up. The context means that Savali, 'the messenger,' was sent down to summon a fono or council of the gods whose stations had been appointed in the various heavens below, and tell them that they should go up to the Ninth Heavens to deliberate there. This was a council of chiefs, for these gods are called ali'i, 'chiefs.' The fono determined to send Savali down with a message to Night and Day. (p. 14)

[25] Langi-uli, 'the dark, cloudy heavens;' Langi-mā, 'the bright clear heavens,' called also Langi-lelei (lelei, 'good, beautiful'). Uli means 'black,' 'dark blue.' (p. 14)

[26] Last injunction; mavaega, 'a parting command.' (p. 14)

[27] Manu'a and Samoa. The pride of the race comes in here; Manu'a is the child of Night and Day, and is the brother of the Sun and Moon. The ruler of the 'Celestial Empire' even cannot claim a more ancient lineage than that! (p. 15)

[28] Sa-tia-le-moa. On this fabulous account of the origin of the names Samoa and Manu'a, Mr. Powell's MSS. have this note:—This affair of the names is in a very confused state. A man, Taua-nu'u, who is 'keeper of the traditions' for Taū, told me lately that Tangaloa fell from a precipice on to Malae-a-Vavāu, and was badly wonnded, and from

that circumstance Tau was called Manu'a tele, 'greatly wounded.' Several persons told Mr. Pratt and myself, in 1862, that the whole group is named Sāmoa, from Moa, the family name of the present King of Manu'a—Sāmoa or Sā-moa-atoa. Fofo and Taua-nu'u still maintain that the account given to Mr. Pratt and myself is perfectly correct, and that le atu o Moa ('the Moa group') includes Samoa, Tahiti, &c., &c.

You two also; i.e., the father and the mother with their four boys.

Malae-a-toto'a. It is a peaceful region, a land of rest and tranquillity; it is the glassy empyrean, beyond the reach of storms. (p. 15)

[29] Builders; 'tūfūga.' see the 'Solo o le Va.'

Bright house. This paragraph seems to mean that the palace in the Ninth Heavens was not their work, although they built in all the heavens below. Fale-'ula* is the 'bright house'; fale, 'a house,' 'ula, 'red,' 'joyful,' 'bright'; hence the name means 'house of joy,' or 'the house beautiful.'

Offspring of Fatu and 'Ele'ele. All the children of Earth are placed under the command of these two chiefs, Manu'a and Sāmoa.

Tail of the names. Chiefs often have the name Tangaloa as the last part of their own names.

Tui, &c., 'King of great Manu'a and all Sāmoa.' Tui also means 'king,' 'high chief.' (p. 15)

[30] Follow. The sun and the moon are not here the cause of day and night; they only follow them. The day breaks, then comes the sun; darkness falls, and ere long the moon rises Shades; ata, 'shade,' 'emblem.' The 'ata' or 'spirit' of Tangaloa resides in them, as in the Tuli; see note on par. 22.

Portion of the heavens; itu, 'side,' see notes on par. 20. The moon and the stars always pass along the sky in the same direction. (p. 16)

[31] Went to and fro; 'fe-alu-alu-mai'; cf. notes on par. 13. To visit the lands; 'asi-asi i nu'u.' Here Savali performs the functions Tangaloa asi-asi nu'u, another manifestation of the supreme god; in visiting these lands he assumed the form of the Tuli; cf. the 'Solo o le Va.'

The Eastern groups; that is, Tahiti and the adjacent islands.

The space between; 'vasa,' that is, the ocean-space between two islands.

Walk it; 'savali,' in allusion to his name.

Turned his face; fa'asaga, 'to direct to,' 'to face to.'

The Tongan group; which is placed as a steppings-stone between the Eastern group and Fiji. That land; 'lau-'ele'ele'; see note on par. 13. (p. 16)

[32] This Manu'a; the land of the poet's birth.

Move about; 'fe-alu-mai,'—not the frequentative form this time. The meaning is that Manu'a was too small an island, and so the land ('lau-'ele'ele') of Savai'i was created. Therefore in poetry, these two islands are regarded as proceeding from the same act of creation. (p. 16)

[33] Got countries; nu'u, 'lands.' Tangaloa, the supreme god, now goes down to examine the lands just created. Cf. "And behold every thing that he had made was very good." Delighted in them, 'fia-fia,' intensive; said, 'fetala'i,' a chief's word.

Black cloud; 'ao-uli-uli'; this is not a rain-cloud; in the book of Isaiah (c. iv., 5), the day-cloud, which is a manifestation of Jehovah's presence, a cloud of smoke ('anân v'âshân); cf. also 1 Kings, viii., 10.

Trample upon;† 'soli-soli,' reduplication. As man is now about to come on the scene, the supreme god prepares the land for him to dwell in and to cultivate.

People to possess; lit., 'people to people,' tagata e faʻa-tagata.

Atu-sasae; 'atu' means 'group,' and 'sasae' means 'eastern.' Atu, Sasae, Fiji, Tonga, are all personified here and become mythical personages. Here, as elsewhere, Fiji, although Melanesian, is included in the realms of Tangaloa, the Eastern God. (p. 16)

[34] Valuʻa and Tiʻapa; these heroes are celebrated in another Solo.

Iʻi and Sava; a myth to account for the name Savaiʻi. Mr. Powell's notes add:—"Such is the account given me by Taua-nuʻu of Manuʻa, the legend-keeper (Oct. 21, 1870). He also stated that Fatu and ʻEleʻele were the first pair who came from heaven; they came down at a place called Malae-a-Vavau, near the east end of the village of Taū; they gave birth to a boy and a girl named Tiʻapa and Valuʻa who went and peopled Savaiʻi; for they became the parents of a girl named Iʻi and a boy Sava; hence the name Savaiʻi."

This side of the world; 'lenei itu lalolagi.' (p. 17)

[35] As if he were making a prayer; 'peiseai se talo-talo ua fai'; talo-talo is an intensive reduplication of the verb tatalo, 'to pray'; talo-saga is 'a prayer'; talo means 'to make signs to,' 'to beckon'; hence 'to stretch out the hands in prayer.'

Land of Upolu; Tutuila; 'land' here is lau-ʻeleʻele, not nʻu.

To rest; malolo, 'to be quiescent,' 'to rest,' not 'to rest from work'; lands, nuʻu. (p. 17)

[36] The Peopling Vine; le Fue-tagata; cf. the 'Solo o le Va,' (note 16). Evidently this vine has some connection with the Sun.

A council ground; that is, a malae.

Was walking; eva-eva, not fe-alu-alu-mai; eva means 'to walk by moonlight,' 'to walk or go about leisurely.' His work was done, and so he could now take a stroll for recreation.

Shred them; 'totosi;' tosi means 'to tear in strips,' though not so as to separate; 'to draw out,' 'to form.'

Four persons; a myth to account for the names Upolu tele and Tutuila

Fue-sā, 'the sacred climbing-vine.' Here called also Fue-tagata—an additional particular, not mentioned in the 'Solo o le Va.'

Flat lands; lau-'ele'ele. Parting command; 'mavaega.' (p. 18)

[37] Show respect to; 'le sopoia;' lit. 'do not pass over.'

Do as he likes; pule, 'have authority and full control.' (p. 19)

[38] As is usual, the poet, at the close of his tale, enforces the claim of Manua, to have glory and honour. (p. 19)

[39] Parallels to these are found in others of our Samoan myths. (p. 20)

[40] Parallels to these are found in others of our Samoan myths. (p. 20)

[41] Parallels to these are found in others of our Samoan myths. (p. 20)

[42] Parallels to these are found in others of our Samoan myths. (p. 20)

[43] Parallels to these are found in others of our Samoan myths. (p. 20)

www.ingramcontent.com/pod-product-compliance
Lightning Source LLC
Chambersburg PA
CBHW051554010526
44118CB00022B/2706